WHERE ARE YOU
ADAM?

"And the Lord God called unto Adam and said unto him,
Where art thou?"

FOREWARD BY RICHARD L HOLT
FORMER NAVY SEAL

WHERE ARE YOU
ADAM?

ABRAHAM?   DAVID?   ANDREW?   MALCHUS?

JOYCE CARR STEDELBAUER

TATE PUBLISHING
AND **ENTERPRISES**, LLC

Published by Tate Publishing & Enterprises, LLC
127 E. Trade Center Terrace | Mustang, Oklahoma 73064 USA
1.888.361.9473 | www.tatepublishing.com

Tate Publishing is committed to excellence in the publishing industry. The company reflects the philosophy established by the founders, based on Psalm 68:11,
"The Lord gave the word and great was the company of those who published it."

Book design copyright © 2012 by Tate Publishing, LLC. All rights reserved.
Cover design by Shawn Collins
Interior design by Chelsea Womble

Published in the United States of America

ISBN: 978-1-61862-687-5
1. Poetry / Subjects & Themes / Inspirational & Religious
2. Religion / Christian Life / Men's Issues
12.05.04

DEDICATION

In memory of my father,
Daniel Murray Carr.
Thank you for a good beginning,
thank you for your appreciation
of the printed word,
thank you for the last, fleeting
"I love you."

And always, my husband,
George.

Acknowledgments

"I'm thanking you, God, from a full heart.
I'm writing the books on your wonders.
I'm whistling, laughing, and jumping for joy:
I'm singing your song, High God."

Psalm 9: 1 The Message

Steve and Teresa Kauffman helped format the manuscript with careful attention to detail. I am deeply indebted to them for their patience, understanding, and especially their friendship. During that time Steve suddenly became critically ill. With his doctors' wisdom and many prayers on his behalf, The Lord has returned him to full strength.

Once again Tate Publishing has produced a book to show forth this ancient and always timely message that God continues to seek us individually so we may know and trust Him personally. The staff are outstanding in their dedication, expertise, and desire to honor the Lord. I have depended on them and found them to be most helpful and efficient. Thank you, Jessica, my faithful editor. And thanks to Chelsea and Shawn for your design and guidance.

TABLE OF CONTENTS

FOREWORD

If you are looking for a book of poetry, forget it, this isn't one. Joyce Stedelbauer has used poetic license to write this book about men without the slightest care of what we may have known as poetry heretofore. I've had to contain my mirth as I have read this collection drawn from the Scriptures. Right from the outset of *Where Are You Adam?* through the wifely attack and interrogation of *Zacchaeus…You short straw!…You squashed fig!…You stunted stick!* you will chuckle with laughter as you read these lines by Joyce. What a gift God has given this girl—maybe *lady* now (we met in high school)—to take mere words and make them exciting in this book.

Most of you, like me, skimmed over the name of *Jarius* in Luke 8—that name not leaving much of an impression. In fact I could not remember who he was. I went back to the Bible to find out. The story around him did stick in my head, but not the man. But when Joyce gets into this man's story and places him at a key spot in the ministry of Jesus in such a way as to bring him out of hiding, it really changes my vista on this chapter of the Bible. It brings the healing ministry of our Savior into real life. But before the miraculous healing takes place, Joyce brings into the picture some pigs. What pigs, you ask? Well I had to go back to Luke 8 to find that Jesus had just driven a host of demons out of a man and cast them into a herd of pigs that ran down the hill and were drowned in the lake. How many of you remember that part? I remembered some pigs! Well Joyce skillfully weaves the pigs into the story. *Did you hear what happened to all of those pigs?* Sure enough, it was there. I had forgotten.

Or how about *Jonah*? Did you ever hear of the Big Fish Inn? You even get the measurements of the throat and mouth of a sperm whale and that they travel in the Mediterranean. Did you know that another man was rescued alive from the belly of a harpooned whale in Asian waters?

These are but a few of the many stories about men in the Bible that Joyce Stedelbauer has woven into a fascinating storybook of poetry. But the real poetry is the magic in her mind of taking Biblical men, both great and small, and presenting them to us in an enjoyable fashion. You can't put this book down, once you begin. It will amuse you, teach you, and challenge you to consider the men of the Bible in a very different way.

It is my deepest privilege to be able to recommend this wonderful book.

—Richard L. "Dick" Holt
Physicist-Aerospace Technologist
Former Navy Seal

INTRODUCTION

You are Adam. I am Eve. We each are faced with challenges; we make our choices and live with the consequences. I have been studying the Bible for many years and it continually surprises me. It is so real, so down to earth, so accessible through the lives of the men and women who have become my role models. They too faced frustrations and failures, progress and pleasures in their journeys.

Often ideas for the settings of poems come as the result of the travel that my husband and I have been privileged to enjoy, or even here at home at a dinner party. We like to ask a question of our guests, somewhere between dessert and coffee, as to whom they would like to invite to join us around our table. We leave it wide open. Male or female, living or dead, from any era; suddenly, we have symphony conductors, politicians, artists, authors, military heroes, and sometimes a biblical man or woman in the mix. Always new, stimulating conversation is generated. Pat Cummings, experienced in Young Life and church ministry, brought

Malchus to the table and said that he always wanted to ask him if he could hear better out of the ear that Jesus healed. Immediately, I said, "Thanks, Pat—there is a poem in that!"

We were on a Vision trip with International Cooperating Ministries in China and fellow traveler, Robert Leatherwood, also an author, was interested in what I was writing. His question to me was about Demas. "Have you written about Demas? Why do you think Demas deserted Paul?" I depend on friends like these and many more who enrich our lives so generously.

In this little volume, I have chosen a variety of men, both obscure and famous, who people the pages of the Bible. My purpose is to meditate on how these men who lived so long ago faced the circumstances of their lives and what they might be able to teach me. I do understand that God deals differently with each individual and I have much to learn from these mens' lives. In the first book, *Have You Met Eve?*, I asked many of the same questions of Biblical women. I invite you to consider a woman's viewpoint in these brief sketches, then look up the noted reference, read their stories and ask yourself, *Where are you, Adam?*

—Joyce Carr Stedelbauer

When God Whispers Your Name
—Max Lucado

Where Are You, Adam?

Where are you, Man? The Voice that calls is not strident, but it is persistent.

Where are you? Are you still in the sack, head buried beneath the pillows, catching 40 more winks?
Or are you already out jogging in the still sleeping neighborhood, chasing fresh air?
Perhaps you are flying out the front door, coffee in hand, perfunctory kisses for the wife and kids, racing to join the commuter crush.

Are you hunched over a desk, head in hands, in the eternal triangle, wrestling with today's problems?
Maybe you are pacing the factory floor with an eagle eye on the complex machines.
Do you face a room full of restless students or a courtroom of angry people, or a counselor's office with an unhappy man and woman?

Where are *you*?

The Voice is not calling because He can't find you, He is asking so that you can find yourself.

God's first question to the first man, Adam,
"*Where are you, Adam?*"

God was expecting you to meet Him again in the twilight garden but something had changed…
you had been challenged and had made the wrong choice…
so welcome to my world…

ADAM

Adam, suddenly your strong, young shoulders
were freighted with fear,
dismay clutched your heart like a vise,
strange apprehension weakened your limbs.
Wiping juice from your chin,
you yelled at the woman, to
"hurry up!"

You could not restrain the twilight,
fast falling like your spirit.
This was usually your favorite time of day,
when the Lord God came to walk
and talk with you in the cool, green garden.
Frantic—trying to tie on those damn leaves,
you shouted louder, cursed under your breath.
The snake recoiled into the shade of the
Tree of Life.

Then the Voice,
not strident,
but persistent…

Where are you, Adam?

Genesis 3

WHY ABRAHAM, DAVID, ANDREW, AND MALCHUS?

Why not? The first letters of their names spell ADAM. and Adam means *man*. Together they are a good cross-section of mankind.

Abram, the wealthy landowner and businessman, was called by God to leave an idolatrous society. The Lord God changed his name to Abraham and made him the father of a new nation, the Hebrews.

David, the shepherd boy, was chosen by the prophet Samuel to prepare for leadership in music, poetry, war, and politics. He became the finest king of the Hebrew nation.

Andrew, the fisherman, encountered the revolutionary Rabbi who challenged him to become the first of His Disciples. He followed Jesus all the way to the cross and afterwards died a martyr's death for his faith.

Malchus, Caiphas's servant, confronted this Rabbi, to arrest Him and was himself healed after the loyal Peter slashed off Malchus's ear to defend his Master, Jesus.

Abraham believed in the Messiah.

David was promised the Messiah.

Andrew found the Messiah.

Malchus was healed by the Messiah.

These four men are a microcosm of the human condition, and millions more men and women—the rich and poor, the young and old, the slave and free whose lives were maximized after they met Jesus, The Messiah.

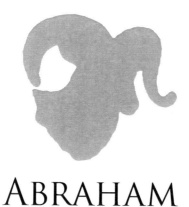

ABRAHAM

Abraham looked up and there in a thicket he saw a ram caught by its horns. He went over and took the ram and sacrificed it as a burnt offering instead of his son.

Genesis 22:13

Abraham Believed the Messiah

By faith, Abraham, when he was called, obeyed by going out to a place which he was to receive for an inheritance; and he went out, not knowing where he was going.

Hebrews 11:8

ABRAHAM

Abram, I remember when we were married, according to custom, when I was still Sarai, before God changed our names. There were many questions in our long life together for which I never found the answers. You knew that I didn't want to move away from Ur. We had a very comfortable life there. I liked the society. It was hard for me in the desert, but I loved you. And we wanted a baby so badly. Then those three mysterious men came that day to our tent. And I laughed. We certainly had our ups and downs, I guess all marriages do. But Isaac was our joy. I almost died when you took him away on that long journey to Mt. Moriah. I never really understood what happened there…

> A resolute man, crowned with age,
> and the sapling youth
> faced the forbidding mountain…
> It stood silent, with a terrible grace,
> as if waiting for countless centuries.

Soft sand of the three-day journey
hardened into sun-struck stone;
the sky a relentless blue tent, no tree offering solace,
no breeze to cool a fevered brow.
They shared a deep draught of well-water
from the goat-skin bag.
He hoisted the firewood onto the boy's back.
Father, where is the lamb?
God will provide, my son.

Tears stung his eyes like a sirocco wind,
ran down the gray beard like anointing oil on a priest.
Unforgiving rocks bruised sandaled feet.
They began the painful ascent.
Air seemed sucked from his lungs.
The peak was as distant as the gates of Heaven.

Another resolute Man, thorn-crowned,
stumbled against the mountain of terrible grace.
It stood, silent, as if waiting for measured centuries.
The city streets around the mountain pulsed with people,
their shouts striking like lethal stones on the Man
who spoke of three days hence.

The sky a bruised banner, no breeze
to cool a bloodied brow,
no tree except the one borne on His beaten back.
Tears of forgiveness ran down His matted beard,
anointing oil on the crucified Priest.

An unlikely mountain to be called
The Joy of the earth,
not spectacular, snow-covered, nor green-robed,
but a rocky ridge rising from the surrounding valleys.
A chosen height for Abraham's altar of obedience,
a threshing floor for the winnowing of grain,
a worship site, a judgment hill, a battlefield,
a crossroads of controversy, and one day,
Mt. Zion, joy of the whole earth.

Genesis 22
Psalm 48

Great is the Lord, and most worthy of praise,
in the city of our God, his holy mountain.
It is beautiful in its loftiness,
the joy of the whole earth.

Psalm 48:1

Ishmael

At eighty-six, you were born to Abraham. He was understandably impatient to have the son that God had promised to him and his aged wife Sarah. When there was no sign that God remembered, Sarah suggested that Abraham visit Hagar, her faithful Egyptian handmaiden, as was sometimes an accepted practice in order to produce heirs. But this was man's solution, not God's plan. Ishmael, your name was announced by the Angel of the Lord, who prophesied your name to be that of *"A wild man, your hand against every man, and his against you."* The Angel also promised that you would become a nation of 12 strong princes.

Scripture declares this and one thing more…

The sun was as high as joy.
Dancing music graced the air,
aromas of roasting lamb, spices, coffee,
dates, figs, bread warm from the fire on the feast day,
celebrating the weaning of Isaac, the son of promise.

28

You, Ishmael, the much loved older son were mocking—-
mocking your father and his young son.
Wild, willful, mean-spirited, dishonoring
the very one who gave you life.
Expelled from their sight, homeless in the desert,
could you have been forgiven if repentant?

Ishmael, you have fathered sons, princes, nations, noble men.
But many sons today still bear your heritage,
Wild as the donkey which cannot be tamed,
hands against every man and every man's hand against you,
despising the sons of the promised Messiah.
Will you still be blinded when He comes again?

I saw you dancing in the streets, celebrating
as firemen strangled to death in the new world holocaust—
slapping your brother's back as men and women
jumped to their doom,
your smiles broad as the terror spreading
like fire around the world—
shouts of glee as the mighty towers crumbled into coffins,
the ink not yet dry on payments to the bombers' families.

Mocking, mocking Ishmael, Arafat, Mohammed Attar.

Genesis 16

Isaac

Frequently in Scripture, we see a record of God changing a name from what a man was naturally in himself, to what he could become by transforming power. Jacob, the deceiver, became Israel-—the heir of the covenant. Cephas, the ordinary fisherman, became Peter—the rock upon which God would build his church. The murderous Saul became Paul—the first great missionary of the faith. Today our names have the additions of titles or degrees, but more often we speak of character traits when we say, "He is a changed man." We know that the most effective and lasting change is when a man truly encounters the living Christ. But the amazing fact of the Bible is that it shows us ourselves in the varied stories and parables. As Paul reminded young Timothy, *All Scripture is profitable for us.*

Isaac of the first family of the covenant people, did you ever wonder why God never changed your name? You were always laughter—always laughter from your aged mother's chortle when the angel promised your birth.

She had been Sarai, meaning contentious, before she was a pregnant Jewish princess. Abram, your father, became Abraham, the father of many nations, after the covenant sealed by fire.

I imagine you with quicksilver feet
avoiding the taunts and threats
of scheming Ishmael, your bastard brother.
You were trained in the shade
of your father's black goatskin tent,
welcomed into the precise ritual
of coffee beans roasted over an olive wood fire
and ground with a metal mortar and pestle
into a pungent powder.
The distinctive *chink, ca-chink, ca-chink*—
a call to all men within hearing to come for coffee.
You listened to talk of herds and bartering and
rode camels to market in Beersheba on Thursdays.
Today you would still be able to visit
your father Abraham's old well.
You loved sleeping out under the blanket of stars,
wrapped in your leather cloak.
You became a man of God on Mt. Moriah,
obedient bearer of your own wooden cross.
Did laughter not fail you then?

Laughter had flowed into a deep river of joy
after you saw the ram caught in the thicket.
When the beautiful Rebecca came home to your mother's tent
and finally bore you twin sons,
you knew true thanksgiving once again.
But she took advantage of your dim sight in waning years,
plotted with Jacob, her favored son,
to trick the privileged blessing from your hand.
Deception haunted your life.

Twelve strong grandsons vied with each other,
laid a bloodied robe in Jacob's lap.
Laughter through pain, laughter in spite of pain,
laughter through tears—
that day in Egypt at the reunion
that God meant for good.

Genesis 22

"Father?"

"Yes, my son?" Abraham replied.

"The fire and wood are here, but where is the lamb for the burnt offering?"

"God himself will provide the lamb for the burnt offering, my son." And the two of them went on together.

Genesis 22:7,8

JACOB

Jacob, the deceiver. What a terrible nickname to haunt you through life. Worse than all of the other names which boys use to disparage each other. This one was yours from birth, and you lived up to those implications. Life had never seemed to work out the way you had planned. And yet we remember you as one of the three fathers of Israel. Because God never goes back on His Word, He did pass the Covenant on through you as He had promised Abraham and Isaac.

I imagine you sitting under a palm tree,
its fronds limp and broken
after a long and windy life.
Your twin Esau was a constant storm
blowing in the wrong direction.
Cheating him out of his birthright
might have seemed like a great trick but
then your uncle Laban gave you a taste
of the same kind of stew.

Mandrakes and speckled goats,
the wrong bride in your tent,
you could not have written such a story,
but you lived it, on through the bloody robe
that aged you beyond your years.

A deep hunger gnawed at you throughout
the golden years of family and friends.
It was hard to see why God had changed
your name to Israel, the covenant name.
How could you be the father of a nation when
you couldn't even keep your own family together?

Now, here at the end of an arduous journey,
you resigned all authority and blessed
Ephraim more than Manasseh,
as Joseph had required.
Why was life so hard to withstand,
like the relentless sun of Egypt
that burned the branches of the palm?

Genesis 48

JOSEPH

Did your brothers call you "Little Joe" and "Daddy's boy" when they ripped the rainbow robe from your young shoulders and threw you in the pit of a dry well? Conscience-stricken Rueben prevailed, and they hauled you out after a while and sold you into slavery to traders on their way south in a camel caravan.

Your biography, Joseph, has traveled from Sunday school classrooms to the Broadway stage, from Pharaoh's palace to prison and back again to the palace to become the chief administrator of Egypt during a most tumultuous time in her long history. Your wise business decisions saved the Egyptians from starvation in time of famine. Your wisdom is needed again today in Egypt.

Even your own family came south in their desperation for food.

You concluded that your brothers *had meant it for evil, but that God intended it for good.*

Languishing in prison, far from home,
you had lots of reasons to be angry:
the betrayal of brothers, Ishmaelite traders,

Potiphar's wife,
seductive as a snake coiled on her pillow,
and the Baker and the Cupbearer.
Days disappeared into weeks,
weeks dried into months,
months crumbled into years.
Hope collapsed into frustration, frustration into longing,
longing finally was resigned to despair.

Where was the God of your fathers,
Abraham, Isaac, and Jacob?
Where was the sand?
Where were the stars of promise?

Suddenly expelled into the sunlight of the Palace courtyard:
challenged with dreams, charged with responsibility,
comforted with a wife and two sons,
confronted with unknowing brothers, you wept.
You began to weave strong cords of reunion
into hope of renewal, renewal into ropes of forgiveness.
Forgiveness anchored a bridge that you crossed,
robed in dignity.

As the prison of death loomed near, you solicited
a promise that countrymen would not
leave your bones in Egypt.
Your bones finally rested in Israel.

Genesis 50

MOSES

Twentieth century explorers, David Cornuke and Larry Williams, believe that they have found the cave on Mt. Sinai where the Lord hid Moses *while His glory passed by!* What must it have been like, Moses, to see God's back? Was it unapproachable light that burns the eyelids shut or a palpable presence felt, not seen? Suddenly your life exploded once again in Howard Blum's bestselling account, *The Gold of Exodus.* Is this the same cave, as the authors suggest, in which Elijah found refuge? Is this mountain the same as Jebel al Lawz in Saudi Arabia, today? Why is it sealed off by the government? What is man afraid to see? Many, of course, understand this to be simply another Bible myth. And we have conveniently removed the Ten Commandments from our school walls so that your name never needs to be remembered. But in 2009, to commemorate the death of pop-star Michael Jackson, the Congress of the United States observed a moment of silence!

Moses, I am stunted by your stature.
My pen reluctant to even trace the shadows
of a man seasoned by miracles—

the Hebrew baby raised to be a Prince of Egypt,
the bush that flamed your obedience,
the rod of God that supported courage,
the sea that stood aside and roared death,
the pillar of cloud that cooled the day,
the fire that torched the night,
the spring that sweetened the desert,
the manna that satisfied hunger,
the mountain cave that protected you
from unapproachable glory.

All of these were created by the shadow
of the hand whose finger carved the stone.
Moses, your prayer has become my prayer.

Lord God, if You are not going with us,
don't let us move a step from this place

Exodus 2

JOSHUA

Gospel groups sometimes still harmonize on the old standard, "Joshua Fit the Battle of Jericho." Joshua was a remarkable man who bore the Hebrew form of the name Jesus. He became a type of the ministry of Jesus as he led the cumbersome, complaining nation of Israel into their new God-given homeland. Joshua had always seen the glass as half full. Born in the desert, nourished on sweet water, manna, and quail, he thrived in the outdoor life. He and his buddy, Caleb, each tried to be the first to see the cloud or fire move. But from the day on the Jordan's riverbank when he swore an oath, *As for me and my house, we will serve the Lord* to the time of his burial on the family estate in Galilee at Timnath Serah, Joshua was a faithful leader. In Israel today, men still study his strategy and name their sons Joshua, even as they long for Messianic peace.

Joshua did you know how blessed you were
to be mentored by Moses?
A man who understood both fortune and failure—
who dealt with all kinds of people "24-7"—
under both cloud and fire,
desert and palm oasis.

Joshua, were you humbled
when he commended you to Eleazer, the priest,
to be charged with the responsibility
of leading the fledgling nation?
Joshua, muscled on manna,
son of the desert wilderness,
faced with the swollen Jordan River,
for your first test—
what did you know of rivers?

Alone, under the canopy of stars,
listening to the voice of the God of the Ark,
you obeyed His every instruction.
The Ark and families and animals
crossed safely between walls of water,
stacked up like the memorial stones
you set carefully for future generations
on a riverbed as dry as the desert
under a fiery sky.

Numbers 27

GIDEON

How would you introduce Gideon at a dinner party?
Some may not know him; another may ask how he put
Bibles in all of those hotel rooms. A soldier will thank
him for the New Testament in his breast pocket that
saved his life when he was shot. Fifth graders used to
receive a copy as a guide for life from the International
Association of Gideons. The records show that millions
of lives have changed course because they encountered
the Living Word, Jesus Christ, in the written Word.
But Gideon was not naturally bold; he was scared to
death—hiding—when
God used an angel to whisper his name.

"Where are you Gideon?
I looked for you when
the dew danced on the threshing floor.
Again when the sun lifted the veil of morning
and the breeze blew away
the last chaff of yesterday."

"Where are you Gideon?
The ox and the ass bleat
and yet you do not come.
The wheat needs to be winnowed
and the Midianites lie in wait like scorpions.
The God of your fathers declares
that He is with you
so fear not!"

"O, excuses, excuses, Gideon,
God has heard them all.
Now I find you down here
in the valley in the winepress,
cringing like a girl. It will never do!
God sent me to tell you
that He is with you."

"O mighty man of valor,
you have a job to do.
Remember,
obedience begins when the way grows rough.
The time of the sweetness of grapes will come
after the altars, after the fire,
after the fleece."

Judges 6

Boaz

Thank God that there are so many men like Boaz, an astute businessman, a law-abiding citizen, and a compassionate friend. He secured a place for himself in the genealogy of Jesus Christ. So often our news focuses on those who murder, rape, and gorge themselves on pornography. But Boaz was a benevolent employer, respected citizen, and loving husband.

You were never a nine-to-five man.
The Elimelech family farms, an all-consuming plan.
Town councilman, seat on the stock exchange,
selling grain futures, respected bachelor of Bethlehem.

Boaz, you had weathered withering days of famine
when capricious Judges ruled the land,
promises like empty clouds mocked the dust.
Refusing to flee as others had,
you stayed to labor in the House of Bread.

She came to your attention, the graceful young widow,
gleaning grain dropped by the reapers in your fertile fields.
Inquiring of her sorry state—no pension plan,

insurance, or social security—compassion
charged your heart, granting permission and protection.

Faithfully she filled her basket under searing sun,
just enough grain—bread for two—Ruth
and her withered Mother-in-law.

The Moon crushed the threshing floor with silver.
Weary from winnowing, you slept.
All pride aside, obedient to Naomi, she crept to
lie at your feet—silently as the stars moved
across the heavens.

Early at the city gate—
sipping first coffee of the day—
you advocated her case.
Slapped a scuffed sandal with the nearest relative
to secure Ruth's future with you.
Love swelled your heart for the virtuous widow.

But Boaz, even you not could see the future
far enough to know that Obed, born
that year to Ruth at the family farms,
would be the progenitor of The Daystar,
which would rise in God's good time
across the threshing floor of Bethlehem.

Ruth

Samuel

As a child I used to feel sorry for you that your mother sent you away from home to study with a priest. Were you a lonely boy? Isolated? No buddies to play with? In such circumstances, many a child has learned to listen for the mysterious call of God. And many have answered with the trusting words of Samuel…

Samuel…
three times the voice had called in a single night.
A voice of authority, not yet understood,
a strong voice, but not fearsome.
The lamp burned low,
the marble floor was cold to bare feet,
shadows whispered on the walls.
Was old Eli awake or asleep?
"Here I am."

He said he did not call you, sent you back to your pallet.
Again and yet again, you dared to tell him
that you had heard your name.

At last the Priest understood, sent you again
to lie down and listen, instructing you how to answer.
Wide awake now, you waited.
The wind hummed in the willows,
a nightingale sang,
a donkey brayed,
and still you waited…

Where are you, Samuel?
You could not know that this same voice
would speak to you for years to come,
of prophets and kings, asses and armies,
altars and the Ark.
Speak, Lord, for thy servant heareth.

Samuel

King Hezekiah

Today as I write this introduction, Egypt is still in chaos. Revolution is the battle cry, enemies face off with home-made weapons, from Molotov cocktails to rocks, and people are desperate to search for food and clean water in order to survive. Only the names have changed from Hezekiah's time, and they will change again tomorrow as new confrontations erupt and threaten to topple our earth from its axis.

O King Hezekiah,
You made the *Washington Post,* September 11, 2001,
ironic, that is also our day of remembering.
King Sennacherib of Assyria mocked you
even as Osama bin Laden
taunted us with acid arrows of hatred.

O King Hezekiah,
engineers today marvel at your tunnel from Gihon Spring
to the city cisterns, assuring fresh water even in times of siege.
They ponder, how did the teams meet
so deep beneath the holy ground of David's city?
Was air bellowed into the blackness
to assuage their sucking lungs?

Desperate clawing marks of iron chisels
still visible on limestone walls today,
to adventurers who wade in the
fresh flow, bending low,
as the tunnel writhes it's way beneath the modern city.

You ruled wisely and well for 14 years until
a serious malady attacked you like an Assyrian chariot.
You pled with God. A brave soldier too soon wounded.
Isaiah the prophet was your confessor.
The sun lingered on the palace steps
as a good sign of God's favor for 15 additional years,
a fact resolving a NASA riddle in recent calculations.

But when royal emissaries from Babylon visited you,
Isaiah asked, *What did they see in your house?*
A poison arrow of pride had found its target.
You displayed all your wealth before the foreigners.
The prophet sadly foretold that Babylon
would carry away all the treasure of Jerusalem.

O King Hezekiah,
may we beware the enemies without and within
as long as God allows the sun to shine on our palace steps.

II Kings 17

Nehemiah

Like many men today, you faced a major career change. The King of Babylon, Artaxerxes, assigned you the arduous task of rebuilding the destroyed wall and temple in Jerusalem. This huge project required new skills which were radically different from your current occupation, with little time to train. You are still respected as a role model today for your courage and dedication against all odds.

The royal title of "Cupbearer to the King"
was suffixed to your name
like the engraved seal on his silver goblets.
An acute sense of taste, honed only on the finest wines,
succulent meats, pristine fruits dripping honey,
and vegetables as colorful as your life.

On silent slippers you moved along the marble
passageways of the fabled palaces of Babylon,
the most trusted Jewish servant.

Suddenly you were freed to go home
and charged with permission
to rebuild the broken down wall surrounding
the temple and the embattled city of Jerusalem.
Cupbearer, the king's sommelier, to construction engineer!
Did you cry out to God for wisdom,
worried that the task was overwhelming?

Exchanging silver goblets for hammer and chisel,
your once fine hands soon hardened to the task.
And it was no easy task,
every man had to defend himself with a sword
in one hand and a trowel in the other.
How did you convince the mayor's daughters
to soil their pretty hands in the dirt and stone?

You knew the clamor of taunting threats,
not of unions and strikes, but Sanballat and Tobiah,
seeking to stop the building project.
But when successfully completed,
joyous music of two choirs, atop the wall,
echoed far across the desert mountains.

Nehemiah

The Winter Banquet Of King Khshayarshan In 483

BC

Historians remember him as Xerxes or Ahasuerus, as he was known in Greek and Hebrew. I am using his name in the Persian language because the following true picture of his realm which stretched from India to Ethiopia is in the very stylized Persian form of poetry known as a ghazal. This form requires exotic language, rich settings, and the author's name must appear in the final couplet.

These couplets may also be read in alternating lines and still convey the story. The following scene is the seventh and final day of the feast when the king ordered his Queen Vashti to his orgy. She refused to come, was banished, and the selection of Esther as his new queen followed. He sent letters throughout his kingdom, stressing that *Every man must rule his home and assert his authority.*

She loved you once, O King Khshayarshan,
when the cool moon was a silver sickle on the hip of night.
You reaped the tender bud of her virginity
before the canopied sky turned to rain.
She was your faithful Queen, ruling from India to Ethiopia,
but burning clouds sailed the roiled seas.
Grand banquets the flourishing signature of the Kingdom,
and the peacock screamed
and the bear danced on…

Your word, O King Khshayarshn, was law in 127 provinces.
The desert wind drove all to Susa, the win-
ter capital beyond the Tigris.
Twenty Satraps waited on the royal
edict, governing by your favor.
The impregnable fortress enclosed the succulent gardens.
You grew fat on figs and dates, sticky
juice clotting your beard,
and stars fell from Queen Vashti's veiled eyes.
You ordered invitations for the feast of the century,
and the peacock screamed
and the bear danced on…and on…

O King Khshayarshan, wine stained your
fleshy lips with purpled pride.
The sickle was sheathed in a pocket of gold.
You commanded Vashti to display her
beauty before the revelers,
under the linen tent tied with violet cords
to silver rings on marble posts.
The Queen refused to parade before the drunken males
in the glow of the lanterns of the orangerie.
King Khshayarshan you denounced her crown;
but Vashti retained her dignity,
and the peacock screamed,
and the bear danced on and on and on…

I know because I, Joyce, was but a serving maid,
spilling the wine
and sweeping broken bottles
from the pictured pavement.

Esther

"If you remain silent at this time, relief and deliverance for the Jews will arise from another place, but you and your father's family will perish. And who knows but that you have come to this royal position for such a time as this."

Esther 4:14

DAVID

I have seen a son of Jessie of Bethlehem who knows how to play the harp. He is a brave man and a warrior. He speaks well and is a fine looking-man. And the Lord is with him.

I Samuel 16:18

David was promised the Messiah

"I, Jesus, have sent my angel to you to tell the churches all those things, I am both David's root and his descendant, I am the bright morning star."

Revelation 22:16

DAVID

Much of the Bible tells the stories of your amazing life. More men are named for you by their praying parents than almost any other name. They are hopeful that their sons would develop many of the finest qualities of your character, so they instruct them in the exciting life of David, king of Israel.

David, how would I dare to write of you…
you, the Poet Laureate of all time?
My most mellifluous metaphor is jangling jargon
beside your *green pastures and still waters,*
my sharpest simile but a bubble before your sword
to slay the wicked.
My most honest attempt at confession, pitiful
compared to the baring of your heart's
shameful deed that haunts day and night.
My major hymn of praise like an infant babbling beside
You, O Lord, are robed with honor, majesty, and light.

You teach me the joy of language,
the privilege of passion, the treasure of tears;
you show me the Messiah.
Some readers may prefer the persuasion of Paul,
others the authority of Peter or the insight of John.
But if the only pages of Scripture I had were just
these few thin, underlined, thumbed, worn,
tear-stained Psalms, it would be enough…

to be *like a tree planted by the river of water,*
to know *that night after night showeth knowledge,*
to sit where *You prepare a table before me,*
to dwell in *Your presence every day of my life.*
Create a clean heart in me,
to live under *the shadow of the Almighty,*
I love your law.
I want to *enter Your gates with thanksgiving.*
Bless the Lord O my soul and all that is within me,
You chart the path ahead of me.

David, because of you, *I pray for the peace of Jerusalem.*
Let everything alive give praise to the Lord,
Hallelujah!

Psalms

Jonathan

A classic friendship grew between two men from oppos-
ing worlds. A brotherhood of strength and trust between
a shepherd boy and a king's son, just preceding the golden
age in Israel. The recent book and movie *The Kite Runner*
depicts such a bond, but unlike Jonathan and David, it was
torn apart by societal pressures. We have our share of such
pressures: the wrong side of the tracks, public or private
schools, professional or laborer, black or white, natural born
or immigrant, high school or college degrees, employer or
employee, rich or poor. Many people face terrible choices
between family loyalties and friends in trouble. A strong
man will make strong choices guided by his conscience if
it has been sharpened like flint on the solid rock.

More friend than brother, more brother than friend,
a covenant sealed with royal robe, belt and weapons of war.
You, Jonathan, the elder, a proven warrior,
defender of the nation,
young soldier of honor and the sweetness of honey.

David, son of Jesse, skilled with sheep and slingshot,
first courted, then feared by King Saul.
Jealousy like fire consumed the tall timber of the Monarch,
David was welcomed no more
at the sumptuous table in the palace.

Jonathan, you had battled the Philistines when David
was still anointing his sheep with oil.
You had tasted vengeance and honey, curses and protection,
as your father struggled for power.
What did you know of the Messiah who would be born
a root out of Jesse?
Saul was angry with you and jealous of David—
by now his own son-in-law—
a sorrowful choice to oppose your father
to protect your friend.
The signal code of arrows pointed the time to flee,
but not before David promised to honor your progeny.
Mephibosheth, your crippled son,
was given a permanent place at David's palace table,
because of brothers' loyal friendship.

I Samuel 13

Nathan the Prophet

Nathan, are you son or grandson of a prophet? Did your father not tell you of the hard life ahead for one who must be bold with bad news? How did you know that the call of God was on your young life? Did the vestry council of elders meet with you to question motives and examine your theology? Was it a vision or the still, small voice that whispered to your soul in the sanctuary of the Spirit? Woe to the ill-prepared who venture heedlessly onto holy ground. Judgment looms ahead for the one who would manipulate the message to be more popular with the congregation. Ezekiel and John were each told to eat the Word. Sweet as it was to the tongue, it was bitter truth in the belly. There is no other truth.

In the beginning was the Word and the Word was with God and the Word was God .
Jesus said…if you continue in my Word, you are truly my disciples, and you will know the truth and the truth will set you free.

A prophet's life is often thankless. Imagine always being the one to carry a warning message to the people or announce disastrous news to the king. Is thanksgiving even possible in the midst of sin and suffering?

Nathan, you must have spent long hours on your knees,
seeking the walking stick of courage
before you went to the court of David—Israel's popular King.
News of his clandestine affair with Bathsheba
reverberated in every bedroom and city gate of Jerusalem.
Was the King inviolate, above reproach, a law unto himself?

You presented a powerful parable to King David
when the Lord said, *Go*.
Inescapable truth humbled David.
He confessed his guilt to you.
It was as painful as the laying down of his crown and armor.
You warned of a bloody sword in the palace,
signing his history in red. But the message
continued that the King's life would be spared,
to fulfill God's purpose for him in his generation.

Nathan, bold prophet of God,
your thanksgiving must have overflowed

when you read and sang the Psalms
which poured from David's pen,
Generous in love—God, give grace!
Huge in mercy—wipe out my bad record.
Scrub away my guilt, soak out my sins in your laundry.
I know how bad I've been; my sins are staring me down.
God, make a fresh start in me,
shape a Genesis week from the chaos of my life.

All forgiven sinners know the cleansing of confession
after the battle to submit the will.
All repentant hearts know peace
from the magnificent mercy of God.
All followers of the Word of God know joy
like the jeweled crown of life.

II Samuel
Psalm 51

The Lord sent Nathan to David. When he came to him, he said, "There were two men in a certain town, one rich and the other poor."

II Samuel 12:1

King Solomon and the Zodiac

When the duties of the throne room are discharged like the rays of spent sun I hurry to my palace roof to study the drama of redemption, played nightly on the darkening stage. My father taught me well of the Ladder of the Heavens, beauty more brilliant than the golden-scarlet veil of the Temple. Since a lad I have memorized the ancient names, even questioned foreign ambassadors to confirm the same truth in their language of the heavens.

The first act must begin with Virgo the Virgin,
the mother of the longed-for Son,
the Prince, the Redeemer.
Libra the Scales weighs the Price
that Covers like burnt offerings.
There rises the Cross, the signpost, high in the panoply
of light.
Both the Coming One and the
Crown stand before Scorpio
the Scorpion, poised to sting Messiah's heel, but
the Mighty One stands ready to crush the attacker.
Sagittarius the Archer has his bow drawn against the enemy,
Draco the Dragon dares to rear his fiery head.

Act two unfolds as night deepens, pulling my robe closer,
I consider Capricorn the Goat, the Sacrifice.
I focus on the star, the Wounded One, and wonder,
will Messiah be wounded before He has won the battle?
Aquarius the Water Bearer pours forth abundant life,
to slake all thirst
and Pegasus the Winged Horse bears good news for all.
Cygnus the Swan sails overhead in another
perfect Cross, representing the Lord to Come.
Silently in the black ocean of mystery swims Pisces, the Fish.
I hear the ancient stories, the Egyptians, once our masters,
call this the Fish of He who Comes. Before me shines
the Crowned King Who Comes To Rule.
I ponder this ineluctable truth.
Could this be Messiah of whom our Prophets speak?
Ancient astrologers tell me Aries is the Lamb,
the Head, the Sacrifice.
O God, my head is spinning!
We sacrifice thousands of perfect lambs yearly,
the smoke cloaking the acrid air.
And there, waiting, lies Cetus the Sea Monster
crowding the dark.
In Hebrew we call him the Rebel, the Chained Enemy.

Now act three commands center stage over Jerusalem.
Stars in their assigned orbits move relentlessly
toward a new dawn.
Taurus the Bull, the Captain, the Leader in Arabic,
with the Pleiades riding high on his shoulder,
charges into the arena to the applause of heaven.
He stops directly opposite Scorpio, the Stinging Satan,
on my planisphere. And there is the first one I
learned as a child, mighty Orion the Hunter.
His is the Foot that Crushes, the Swiftly Destroying One.
He holds a scepter shaped like a third Cross,
I struggle to understand this repeating sign.
Gemini the Twins carry two flaming banners,
the Ruler and the Strong One coming to Suffer.
How can this be? Messiah will be the King of kings
riding on a milk-white horse to victory.
Travelling the elliptic is Cancer the Crab
crawling toward Truth.
The Multitude and the Offspring
are gathered into the Sheepfold,
much as our shepherds have done for centuries.
They include in their dazzling number the Purchased,
Assembled Together, Protected,
all the Possession of Him who Cometh.
At the trumpet of dawn, the Morning Star appears,
I rejoice in Leo the Lion of Judah,
Treading Underfoot, Putting Down the Enemy
and Shining Forth.

O Lord, when I consider the heavens,
the work of thy fingers,
the moon and the stars
which thou hast ordained:
what is man, that thou art mindful of Him?

Psalm 8

Agur

You are a wordsmith of the finest order. The Williamsburg Poetry Guild would invite you to conduct a workshop for us if you were here. You would help us be even more observant and give us exercises to stimulate our imagination. Were there many male poets in your era? Of course we know the ancient writings of the book of Job and the wondrous words of Solomon. We need more men like you to hammer words into pure gold.

Agur, son of Jakeh, the oracle,
there are three questions I would proffer—
yea, four that burn upon my lips:
Why did you not publish a chapbook
of the poetry in your soul?
Where did you learn the wisdom of the wild things?
How did you mature to understand the mysteries of God?
Who told you— perhaps Isaiah's prophecies—
of the name of the coming Messiah?

You state three themes that expand my mind—
no, four that swell within my breast:
The insatiable hungers that consume all generations,
The quartet of wonderful mysteries,
The two pairs of people that stir up strife,
The tiny trio plus one of miniature things to observe.

There are three truths I glean from you—
no, four that strengthen my shield:
The majestic power of our Creator,
The absolute reliability of His Word,
The severe warning of tampering with the Holy Book
And the humble prayer of a disciple.

Since you wrote King Lemuel's description of an ideal woman
that follows in Proverbs 31, I would call you
Agur, the consummate man.

Proverbs 30

Daniel

They say that there is no retirement plan for soldiers of the cross. Your responsibility in Heaven must be to encourage young followers of Christ. We straighten our backs and sing out "Dare to be a Daniel" from the time we first learned to tie our shoes.

The lions were hungry.
Restlessly they nosed the bars
as you were hurled inside the cage.
They circled like a wake of vultures,
ready to devour your healthy flesh,
teeth bared in a vicious snarl,
whiskers twitching a warning,
tongues slathering, ears pricked,
tails waving a victory banner.
The salacious spectators salivated.
The King took to his bed.

You stood tall in the center of the lions' den,
speaking quietly to your God,
as you were in the habit of doing
three times daily by the open window
in spite of the edict of the King.
The naysayers had spied you there,
in your palace suite, and plotted
their jealous revenge over your favor
in the Babylonian court.

The Omnipotent One stroked the furry
backs of the beasts, shut their mouths
as if bound with velvet ropes,
satiated their hunger,
quieted their stalking,
and they lay down at your feet.

Daniel

JONAH

Why include a man that many have relegated to movies and bedtime stories? Some creative skeptics even suggested that a ship named *The Fish* came along at the moment of splashdown. Others came up with the idea that the hapless Jonah crawled ashore, saw the lights of the Big Fish Inn, and stumbled to the door. They claimed that there was no whale whose throat was wide enough to swallow a man, until they measured a sperm whale's throat and found it to be 9 feet by 15 feet by 22 feet. Sperm whales are known to travel Mediterranean waters. In the 1800s, a man was rescued alive, but bleached, from the belly of a harpooned whale in Asian waters. Most importantly, Jesus said that He would be in the grave as long as Jonah was in the now-famous whale.

Jonah, Do you really expect me to believe you…
that absurd tale of waves and whale? I know you sold
your script to DreamWorks and *VeggieTales*,
and yet…and yet…
the scholars of Scripture reserved
your place in the Holy Canon.

DreamWorks must have fabricated your great fish,
the prototype of *Jaws*, larger with each telling,
as animatronic engineers opened and closed
your cavernous mouth, without the pearl pillars
impaling your pride. Absurd!

Jonah, do you really expect me to believe you…
you of the recalcitrant heart who despised your enemies?
How did God make a prophet out of such a
ragged bag of bones with weed-wrapped hair?
You had money enough to buy a ticket to Tarshish,
thinking you could run away from God. Absurd!

Jonah, do you really expect me to believe you…
you survived three dry days in the coral-colored chambers
and three Cimmerian nights to reconsider your call?
And yet…and yet…
The Bible records that your passionate prayer
was met by the mercy of God in spite
of your struggle with anger versus compassion.

Thanks, *VeggieTales*, the gourd and the worm were terrific!

Jonah

Micah the Prophet

The citizens of earth will *drink the wine of astonishment* when they connect the dots that you have spaced out in your prophecy. Like a child's party game, it will be easy to see the pictures outlined, filled in, and colored perfectly. Careful readers will puzzle over having missed the message. If we do not read the instruction manual for life— the Bible—we simply draw our own conclusions and decide that life is a game of multicolored choices. Like balloons at a birthday party, some will explode right in our foolish faces.

Micah, how did you know
those long, crenellated centuries ago?
Was your wisdom written with the ink of age
that we should read your words on a printed page?
Was your visionary insight revealed
on bomb-bright nights
that the United Nations should quote you,
but continue to fight?
Was your discernment so supernaturally understood
that you knew what the Lord requires to do good?

Micah, you served three kings of Judah
as a prophet of God.
Good Kings who heeded advice
to walk humbly with God;
Jotham, Ahaz, and Hezekiah reigned 61 years, loving justice—
the measure of men who serve the Lord of mercy.
Men still look for the day when every king and nation
will beat their swords to plowshares and be brother relations.

Micah, how did you know,
those broken, rusted centuries ago
that the Prince of Peace would be born in Bethlehem,
even Bethlehem-Ephratah in the south,
not Bethlehem in the northland?
Micah, true wordsmith, though your writings are small,
you revealed God's eternal Truth for all
men and nations to make war no more.

On that New York night
the United Nations will bow before
The King of kings and Lord of lords.

Micah

ZECHARIAH

Zechariah, you godly, old fool! Had you labored in the priestly course of Abijah so long— like the moon shadowing the sun— so long you could not comprehend Gabriel's meaning? Did you burn your fingers on the live coals from the altar when lighting the evening incense, no longer igniting prayer heavenward for your beloved, barren Elizabeth? Old eyes widened, blinking at the brilliance, a shielding hand across the tired brow, light penetrating clutched fingers, shoulders shaking at the soft thunder of His Voice…

"Fear not, Zachariah, your prayer is heard."

A rumbling in ears almost closed by time,

"Son—John—joy—
Holy Spirit—Israel—Elijah—"

Delusions of angels, wings whipping wind,
fanning flames, questioning disbelief,
excuses of rationale, holy fragrance,
falling to your knees before the
Cloud of Unknowing.

Shadows leaned against the walls
and still you did not come—you godly, old fool—
struck dumb for disbelief, nine moons to ponder,
does God still speak?

Elizabeth, blooming with righteous pride,
had all the last words
until you finally wrote,
that day of celebration—
the eighth day of your joy—

His name is John.

Luke 1

John the Baptist

Depending on which generation you call yours, "Boomer" or "Me" or "X," you would call John, who was known as the Baptizer, a Tarzan, a George-of-the-Jungle, or a hippie. He was a wild man. He lived in the wild, ate from the wild, dressed from the wild side, and preached wild reforms. He claimed he was not even worthy to untie Jesus's sandals. But the rabbis were clearly teaching that not even a Jewish slave needed to do such menial work.

Because of your witness, John,
Catholics and Baptists, Congregationalists and Presbyterians,
Methodists, and all manner of believers baptize
those who follow the Christ.
You were just a man, no ordinary man,
a strange man. A man of the land, dressed in skins,
surviving on locusts and honey, sleeping under the starry
gospel sky or secreted in a cave
when clouds let down their hail of tears.

Prophets promised one like Elijah would precede
the longed-for Messiah like winter rains soften the earth.
Dr. Luke chronicled your extraordinary birth from Gabriel's
announcement to your untimely death after the dance.
Mary the Virgin attended your mother Elizabeth
through those last laborious months before your
astonished father, the humbled priest, Zechariah,
broke tradition like a common clay cup, and named you John.

Skeptics and Saints call you
The Voice, crying in the wilderness
for repentant sinners to come to the Jordan.
Your pulpit a rock beside a shallow bend in the river.
Sweet water flowed from Mt. Hermon, rising in the north
through the Galilee, coursing past Jerusalem to the
Dead Sea, where there is no forgiveness.

One diamond morning, a window opened in the ark of heaven.
A Dove, pure white, graced the burnt-blue sky,
rested on the dripping shoulder of Jesus of Nazareth
as you lifted Him from the baptismal Jordan.
The voice of God thundered in your ordinary ears.
Your obedient voice proclaimed.
The Lamb of God who takes away the sins of the world.

John, you should have received velvet vestments
and a higher pulpit.
A bronze likeness
could stand on that river rock;
instead
your severed head
was served on a silver platter
at an obscene orgy before a common king.

Jesus pronounced your epitaph,
The finest man born of woman.

Luke

John answered them all, "I baptize you with water, but one more powerful than I will come, the thongs of whose sandals I am not worthy to untie. He will baptize you with the Holy Spirit and with fire."

Luke 3:16

King Herod

The king's fury burned in his breast like a roaring fire, consumed him with anger that this baby should be born in his jurisdiction. He was fearful of an uprising of shepherds and common men—jealous for his throne. He stood on the vast porches of the Antonio Fortress, shaking his fists at the winking stars.

Who named you "Great"?
Certainly it fit your ego, with a golden crown
flashing in the desert sun.
Friend of Tiberius Caesar, ingratiating favor,
building that playground in the north,
Tiberius on the Sea.
A jewel worthy of an Emperor—
a sapphire ringed by emerald hills of Galilee,
heedless that it rested on a graveyard.
Unclean for any Jew, a resort fit for Romans.

Herod, who named you "Great"?
Caesarea, another namesake jewel,
a necklace of light around the throat
of a deep harbor, carefully dredged to provide
safe shelter from the sometimes jealous Sea.
An ingenious double wall to keep out undesirables,
a magnificent amphitheater for amusements played
on a vast stage with the Mediterranean a turquoise curtain.

Herod, you knew how to live well—like a King—
but for those troublesome Jews, always a pain in your pleasure.
Much could be gained by letting them
rebuild Solomon's Temple.
Let them worship their invisible god
and offer smelly sacrifices.
You ordered your finest engineers to level Mt. Moriah's crown,
where Abraham's raised hand was stayed by an Angel.
Laborers leveraged gigantic stones
to build a supporting wall
to the west,
servant stonemasons hewed the
back-breaking building-blocks—
46 years to complete.

"Herod the Great," your crowning achievement —
a popularity ploy, consuming jealousy feeds on such an ego.
Rumors ravaged your dreams,
an infant King to be born of the Jews?
An extraordinary Daystar heralded his birth,
but where could he be found?
No time now for a play in Caesarea,
cancel the weekend in Tiberius,
pretend to seek him for homage,
solicit the traveling astrologers,
summon the swordsmen of the Antonia Fortress
to deal with this threat.
Slaughter the babies of Bethlehem!

Herod the Great, from your grave, do you still hear
Rachel weeping for her children?

Matthew 2

When it was time for the Wise Men to leave, they returned by another way, for God had warned them in a dream not to return to Herod.

Matthew 2:12

ANDREW

*As Jesus was walking beside the Sea of Galiee,
he saw two brothers, Simon called Peter and his
brother Andrew. They were casting a net into the
lake, for they were fishermen. "Come, follow me,"
Jesus said, "and I will make you fishers of men."*

Matthew 4:18,19

WHERE ARE YOU

Andrew met the Messiah

For whosoever will save his life will lose it, but whosoever will lose his life for my sake, the same shall save it. For what is man advantaged if he gains the whole world and loses his soul?

Luke 9:24-25

ANDREW

Were you always in the shadow of your brother Peter?
Always running to catch his pass, fumbling the ball,
never quite measuring up? Did Dad like him best, or
did it just seem that way? He was so quick to make
decisions, so sure, so cocky, well, confident, at least.
And the girls loved him, hung around whenever you
hauled your boat up on the beach. He had bigger mus-
cles than you did, a louder laugh, a wider smile. Yet you
loved him; everyone did.

I like my work.
Sometimes we work all night and catch nothing
but mostly, there are plenty of fish in this rich,
cool water from the snows of Mt. Hermon.
It is hard work, but our bellies are full
and I have time to think and ask questions.
At night far out on the lake, the water is black
as the hour before dawn, and stars burn
like a million oil lamps.
Who fills the chambers with fresh oil,

trims the spent wicks, who lights them?
Where do the stars go when the roaring sun climbs
the eastern hills and burns my back as we beach the boat?

My brother says I ask too many questions.
He says that I live on the cliff of questions,
but he lives on the rock-hard ground of answers.

Mending the nets is tedious…
I wonder how many cords it would take
to bind up my life with a greater purpose?
After they dry in the aching sun, Peter
and I heave and arrange them carefully
back in the boat, ready for tonight's catch.
Finally, dozing in the shade of a big rock,
I wonder about the length of my life,
will anyone important ever know my name…?

I've seen that man before walking the beach…
he called my name…
what could he want of me?

Matthew 4

Peter

How would you introduce Peter at a dinner party?

"There's the guy with the best fish tales, 153 in one night!"

"Bold, impulsive, brash even…you know his mother-in-law lives with them, and everyone always ends up at his house 'cause it's so close to the synagogue…and his wife is a great cook."

"Well, he is an author…of two short pieces, seldom stays in one place, or stops talking long enough to write."

"He left his business abruptly and followed that revolutionary rabbi everywhere, even had him staying in his home whenever he came back to Capernaum."

"He tells miraculous stories—claims to have witnessed most of them—but that tale of him walking on the water—well, you'll have to ask him."

> Why did you challenge the misty apparition
> that sin-black night,
> was it faith or bravado that yelled
> through the keening wind?

WHERE ARE YOU

The spray stung as you strained to see the luminescent form—
straight as a pillar in the Temple—
wild waves breaking against its strength.
Were you feverish or fervent as you cried out,
If it's you…?

But a few hours ago you were sitting in orange-fragrant shade
watching astounded as a crowd—
larger than your whole village—
feasted on a single boy's lunch.
You knew you would follow,
be a disciple of no other teacher.

Was it fear or hope that threw your question to the wind
…bid me come, walking on the water?
You had resolved to do what He did, to try to be at His side.
You had seen miracles that only the Messiah could do,
and it was His voice that just said,
Don't be afraid.

Leaving the safety net of your pitching boat
with sure steps—eyes locked with His—
you did feel the water wash your feet.
You were living a miracle,
just what He said you could do.

A rogue wave struck from behind like doubt—
you looked down,
away from His smiling face,
were sucked under by fear,
like a weighted net.
Lord, save me!

His arm was strong,
voice firm as thunder,
O man of little faith,
why did you doubt me?

The Gospels

Then Peter got down out of the boat, walked on the water and came toward Jesus. But when he saw the wind he was afraid and beginning to sink, cried out, "Lord, save me." Immediately Jesus reached out his hand and caught him. "You of little faith," he said, "why did you doubt me?"

Matthew 14:29,30

PETER'S SON

There seems to be no record of whether Peter and his wife had sons or daughters; however, children were greatly desired in a normal family. Children, especially a son, removed a woman's shame of being barren, and they were lovingly trained to help in the home. Sons were usually taught the family trade in addition to whatever schooling they received. One day at Peter's house in Capernaum, the chosen twelve were disputing among themselves who would be the greatest in this new movement. Jesus called for a child to come to Him and scooped him up in His arms to teach a lesson on faith. I am imagining that this was Peter's son, and in this poem, he is beginning to learn his father's trade.

I was just six, but I remember
as clearly as seeing my face in the sea,
leaning out of my father's boat.
Someday he said he'd take me fishing.
It was long, hard work.
He and Uncle Andrew went out almost every day,
way before light peeked over the mountains.
But that morning the sea was still as a whisper,
it almost looked like you could walk on marble water.
Daddy was teaching me to row the boat.

I was just six, but I remember
I was already hungry before the sun
was as high as the gulls following us.
I squinted my eyes and thought of Jesus
feeding everyone on that mountain
when the sun grew as hot as fire
and no breeze stirred the olive trees.
We searched for shade, but the big people found it first.
Everyone was listening to Jesus.
He had come often to stay at our house.

I was just six, but I remember
one evening when His friends urged him
to send us away, but He stopped,
like a boat becalmed.
His arms were open, big hands beckoned,
a smile played around His mouth
and spread to His eyes.
He looked straight at me—straight
as a good oar on Daddy's boat,
Let the little children come to me.

I was just six, but I knew.
He drew me into His arms like a net, lifted me up,
my heart pounding like thunder
because I knew
Jesus loved even me.

Mark 10

JAMES

You struggled hard to become a man of faith. Growing up in Nazareth, learning the carpenter's trade alongside of Jesus, you clung to your own conclusions, even the townspeople didn't like Him, so He left. You heard stories about Him, stories you could not believe. But as the stories increased, so did the evidence. After the horror of His death and the wonder of the resurrection, you saw Him again. You knew that all the evidence was true. You knew His saving grace was real. When the Holy Spirit came on the wind of fire, your passion to serve was ignited. It was to you that the nascent community of faith looked for guidance. The Jerusalem council respected your leadership, and the Epistle of James is loved by millions of followers. Worldwide, churches memorialize your name, martyred for the faith which you struggled so hard to believe.

As a boy you taunted Him,
wanted Him to snitch an orange or two…
you called Him names,
He turned again, smiled, and looked at you.

As a youth, you mastered ridicule,
You called him names,
He turned again, smiled, and looked at you.

As a man, you considered Him,
was he not your father's son, yet when he
was near, the deaf could hear, the lame could walk,
why all of this miracle talk?
Crucified?
Resurrected?
You called His name,
He turned again, smiled, and shook His head at you.
I too was blind and now I see.
He turned again, smiled, and gave a final nod to me.

Suddenly, His name was everywhere!
In city market and country air,
Teacher, Shepherd, Physician, Water, Bread,
The Way, Truth, Life, led you to write,
Count it all joy.

James

The Apostle John
on Patmos

To be known as the best friend of Jesus, on earth, was an extraordinary privilege. It does not obviate His dear mother, Mary, but allows you special recognition. Two young Galileans, from Nazareth and Capernaum, the carpenter and the fisherman. You, John, were challenged, not commanded. Counseled, not lectured, entrusted, not enslaved. You knew the plan but not the pain. You shared compassion but not the cross, you shared the tension but not the tomb. You knew the Living Word and wrote the written Word.

You watched Him ascend, knowing that in the Father's perfect time, He will return. Then you took His mother home on your strong arm.

Master, Savior, Friend,
I have lived three times as long as you
and yet am still surprised by grace.

The Carpenter and the fisherman, how odd of God;
you of the shop and field and me of the sea,
you crafting plows and yokes, me, mending torn nets,
you from Nazareth, me from Capernaum,
men as different as heaven and earth.

My mother cried when I left home and family business,
but she came to understand—almost.
Your mother cried when I took her home,
she already knew the pain and the plan.

Those three years were the best of life—the miracle years—
traveling, talking, praying, eating, laughing—
remember Zacchaeus's wife, brawling like a hungry donkey?
The woman at the well, flushed cheeks;
Peter walking on the water, sinking again;
the lad with two fish, did you ever wonder
what happened to him? No, you wouldn't need to wonder.
What a good cook Martha was, Peter's mother-in-law too,
but the finest meal of all was your breakfast on the beach!
Even more wonderful than that last supper together,
because you were back with us. I miss all of those brothers.

I could not have guessed it would be Judas until
you dipped bread for him.

Each worship service when I offer,
in these trembling hands,
the bread and wine—your flesh and blood—
I pray that people understand what it cost you
to hang upon that cross for them.

Thank you for that cave on Patmos,
high above the lapis-blue Aegean.
Thank you for that cave, so quiet—
I could hear your voice.
So cold—I could feel your warmth
So lonely—I knew your presence.
So crude—that I longed for the many mansions
you told us about.
So simple—that I saw walls and ceiling
crowded with awesome paintings of battles,
beasts, kings, and angel wings.
So dark—I could see the light of your face
as you walked beside the crystal river.

It won't be long now until I'm with you again,
my Master, Savior, and Friend.
Amen

Revelation

The revelation of Jesus Christ, which God gave him to show his servants what must soon takeplace. He made it known by sending his angelto his servant John, who testifies to everything he saw—that is, the word of God and the testimony of Jesus Christ. Blessed is the one who reads this prophecy, and blessedare those who hear it and take to heart what is written in it, because the time is near.

Revelation 1:1-3

Philip

The first golf course in Israel was built at Caesarea; beautiful links laid out beside the timeless sea. Your golf club at home can refer you so you can play a round and have lunch at this storied course. Phillip, of course, never knew about a hole-in-one or being caught in a sand trap. Certainly he attended the marvelous amphitheater that King Herod built. The astounding acoustics need no amplification to hear the actors down on the stage with the rocky shore as backdrop. Pilate chose to live here too, as if the restless sea would move him closer to Rome. His reserved seat in the grand arena, engraved with his name, now is kept in the British Museum. But tourists can trace the letters of his name on the copy which is mounted outside in the garden of this ancient wonder. You should lunch outside at Charlie's if you can find a table under the flowering vines.

Philip, you must have been reluctant to leave home
in Caesarea when the Spirit of God spoke to you,
and yet you went as quickly as smoke rises.
I have long admired you, the premier example

of how to share your faith in the Living Lord.
You had just been preaching in Samaria,
might have rationalized that you needed rest
when you were told to go all the way to Gaza.
Immediately your fire was rekindled and you
left, not knowing whom you were to meet.

A foreign chariot was rolling down the road from Jerusalem.
The Spirit said, *Go near.*
You ran like flames through dry grass,
asked the Ethiopian in the fine chariot what he was reading.
Isaiah, and how can I understand this with no one to help me?

You began where he was reading
and explained about Isaiah writing about the Messiah.
You never suggested to go back to stories of Adam and Eve,
or Noah, or what his theory was about the great flood.
The gentleman's heart burned with new confidence,
and he asked to be baptized.
Amazing, isn't it, that you passed by a pool of water
on that desert road? And one more miracle, your robe
still dripping from the wonder of new life in the water,
the Spirit lifted you like sparks rise in the wind
and took you home to Caesarea.

Acts 8

NATHANAEL

It is good to have a friend like Phillip, a friend who takes
you to meet Jesus. Your friend explained that Andrew and
Peter had met him first. Jesus had said to them, *Follow me.*
Follow Him where? Jesus had answers for your questions.
As soon as he spoke about the fig tree, that was your sign.
You knew the Prophet Joel talked about the fig tree, and
Jesus said He came to fulfill the law and the prophets.

Nathanael, as a restless young boy,
did you scramble up into the sturdy branches
of the fig tree, your favorite safe house,
hidden in your own verdant world?
Each leaf was bigger than your young face.
You were careful not to bump the budding fruit—
hard, green globes sticking out at all angles.
Peering between the upraised limbs, you shot
arrow questions into the blue bulls-eye:
"What is God?"
"Where is God?
"Does He see me?"

Many afternoons later, when the target blazed white hot,
you would stretch out along the smooth arms of the fig
that outgrew you year by year. The swelling fruit was
as tantalizing as your first kiss:
"Does God know my name?"
"Why can't He be seen?"
"What sacrifice pleases Him?"

Later when you rested after work, you were content
to lean against the trunk of your question tree
in the evening shadows:
"God if you're real, show me a sign."
"Will I just grow old like Moses and die?"
Can anything good come out of Nazareth?

A perfect ripe fig dropped squarely into your open mouth…

John 1

NICODEMUS

The rock carving of the kneeling Christ that I refer to in
the following poem is in the Garden of Gethsemane, near
a door into the Church of All Nations. It is imprinted on
my mind like Rodin's *Gates of Hell* in the sculpture garden
in Paris which holds some of his most famous work. These
two timeless works of art, the first small and the latter large,
cause me to meditate on the terrible price that Christ paid
on our behalf when He prayed for us and suffered the cross.

Nicodemus, I see you in the shadows.
You, you who came by night as all seeking sinners do,
out of the dark depths of self—
murky motives—wrapped
in a midnight cloak, hiding from pious fellow Pharisees,
slipping soundlessly out of empty streets, stumbling
on the rocky path across the treacherous Kidron Valley
to the garden, the green olive-sweet garden mountainside.
You watched Him kneeling, draped over a
rock in anguished conversation with His Father;
Peter, James and John asleep.

You had noticed His tenderness toward the sick,
listened to audacious claims of Divinity,
watched Him teaching in the Temple,
and so you came,
burdened with the weightiest question of all humanity.
The pivotal question
on which planet Earth tilts on its axis.
The answer unites man and his Maker eternally.
You must be born again.

Nicodemus, I see you at the cross
late in the grey-grief afternoon.
Women weeping, soldiers sleeping, disciples fleeing,
and yet you came,
wrapped in a sorrowful cloak, helping your companion,
Joseph of Arimathea slip the body soundlessly
from the humbled tree—
stumbling under the precious weight, to a garden,
a green olive-sweet garden with a new tomb.

I see you in the Duomo in Florence
on a Son-light morning, standing under Bruneleschi's dome.
You, you, immortalized by Michelangelo
sculpting his features in your marble face.
Palpable sorrow and eternal praise
chiseled together in the passionate Pieta,
polished centuries after the Tomb was empty.

John 3

JAIRUS

Jairus, everyone thought that you had a good "in" with God. That's why they elected you as ruler of the synagogue. They hung around with you because they hoped some of that "good favor" would rub off on them. Nothing bad ever happened to you, probably because you prayed a lot and went to all of those religious meetings.

"Did you hear about Jairus?"
"No, what? Did he earn another good attendance pin?"
"That teacher healer, Jesus, just came back to town."
"I thought He was across the lake—did you hear
what happened to all of those pigs?"
"Yeah, well anyway, there was a big crowd pressing around
to get a look-see, and there right on the dusty road,
Jairus fell face down, right at Jesus's feet."

"What happened—did he get pushed or faint?"
"No way—he just bowed all the way down and said
something about his daughter being really sick."
"O, that pretty little girl—

must be about eleven or twelve by now,
Jairus dotes on her."
"What dad wouldn't…?"
"They don't make them any sweeter,
so what happened?"

"Well they started toward his house but it was slow going,
a lot of commotion in the crowd,
some woman got in their way."
"Figures, that's nothing new…"
"Let me finish. Just before I lost sight of them a servant
came running up and said the little girl was dead!"
"No, that's awful!"
"But wait, Jesus told Jairus, 'Don't be afraid,
trust me, and she will be all right.'"
"Believe, trust?"
"My faith would have been ground down in the dust by then,
but they kept on going—right to his house—
I guess to console his wife."
"I guess sometimes faith does let you down, Poor Jairus,
he won't be praising God all the time now."

Luke 8

LUKE

Dear Dr. Luke:

Your writings interest me, therefore I am writing to request
a consultation in your office. Will I find it on the street of
the Prophets?
You write with great authority of what has already happened.
I understand you traveled extensively with the Apostle Paul.
Did you know him first as Saul?
Can the medical profession affect such an amazing trans-
formation of the spirit?

And what do you know of Jesus of Nazareth? Perhaps you
were a wedding guest when wine was sweeter at the end
than the beginning—is that within your alchemy?
Or were you in Alexandria or Rome at your studies while
these miracles exploded like shooting stars across our land?

Did you witness the Resurrection or even a healing—has
such lightning ever fired your fingertips? How could that
woman who touched Him have bled for a dozen years—
poured out her very life like rain on a dusty road?

WHERE ARE YOU

O, I must apologize, kind sir. I sound as if I am interviewing you. What I meant to do was set forth three questions that trouble me, for your consideration before we meet, if you will indeed do me the honor since I am but a humble woman.

You will find my needs are more of the spirit than the body.

I appreciate your fine reputation of treating the whole person, not just the symptoms.

Please indulge me my questions.

1. Where is the seat of faith—in the mind or in the heart?

2. Why is it that enthusiasm can spike like fever and fall so quickly in the face of opposition?

3. How am I to deal with my desire, like a rising thunderhead, to be made new, transformed, by a process I do not understand?

My young nephew will wait for your reply. Please, good Dr. Luke, if you will be so kind as to see me as an anxious patient needing your healing touch. For my malady is of the spirit if not the body.

Faithfully yours,
Alegria
14th day of Nissan

Acts

THE DEMONIAC

Today, if you read Lauren Hillenbrand's true account of *Unbroken: A World War II Story of Survival, Resilience, and Redemption*. it is not hard to believe in demons. The unspeakable crimes against humanity that it chronicles could only come from the realms of unadulterated evil. Teen books and movies thrive on witches, vampires, ghosts, and otherworldly creatures. Missionary stories often include firsthand experiences with both angels and demons. It is interesting that in this text and others, the demons knew the true identity of Jesus. Both Mark and Luke note that the result of the demoniac meeting Jesus was that the townspeople who knew this tormented man found him *sitting at the feet of Jesus, clothed and in his right mind*.

A head like a small hill pocked with holes.
Rheumy eyes rolled like a wild animal
searching a cave for cover.
Two smaller openings dripped like rusty water
from an old pipe.
Two more coiled like a serpent's tail

spiraling into doom—
The terrain of the hapless hill
was bristled and fissured.
The largest hole gaped raw,
black spaces between broken shards.
Many smaller caves were green as a moonless night.
This is where they lived—

Huddled in greasy gloom, dart-
ing from room to room—
Doubt chased Despair and pinned Fear in a far corner.
Hysteria hounded Shriek in merciless circles
until it escaped the gaping hole.
Worry worked Anxiety and
Discouragement into Desolation.
Rasping Voices echoed from hallways,
bounced back from the walls—

Helpless!
Friendless!
Hopeless!

Then Jesus happened by…

Mark 5

BEAUTIFUL BEGGAR

In the 1950s, Rosalind Rinker wrote a wonderful book about how Christians really share their faith most effectively—"It's when one beggar tells another beggar where to find bread." In our affluent society, it is very difficult for us to see ourselves as beggars. Beggars don't live in fine houses, drive Corvettes, and wear three-piece suits—or do they? Those whose other home is the sport club don't consider themselves as crippled and lame. Those who have an office in which to work don't depend on friends to pick them up bodily and carry them to the supermarket entrance and set them down to beg for handouts. Yet when it comes to sharing the Good News about a vital relationship with Jesus Christ, it is often most meaningful, man to man, face-to-face, because one is truly a starving beggar in dirty rags if he has not tasted the Bread of Life.

Who carried you every day to the gate called Beautiful—
compassionate brothers or profiteers of your pain?

There you waited,
a heap of crooked bones—lying on the path to worship.
You knew them by their feet—
those dusty feet having traveled miles of rough
roads to enter God's house,
dainty feet of the women relegated to their separate court,
bending low to lay their generous offering
in the trumpet-shaped horn.
The well-groomed feet of the wealthy
in smooth, leather sandals,
carelessly tossing in a handful of musical coins
as they paraded past
with never a downward glance to the beggar below.

There were the feet of the two men who spoke daily
in the shade of Solomon's colonnade.
You cried out for money—
they offered mobility,
you begged coins—
they bartered compassion,
you pled mercy—
they searched your face for faith.
They spoke the name of the Great Physician
as they offered a hand to help you stand.

Joy coursed through your shaky body
like new bones for a tired frame.

Acts 3

THE CRIPPLED MAN

If Jesus happened by your desk today, what do you think
He would say to you? "How's it going, you doing okay?
How's the family, kids must be big by now? Sure haven't
seen you for a long time. Job okay? Things are tough all
over—sorry you missed out on the promotion. Heard you
were sick a while back, too. Nothing serious, I hope. I
joined the new gym in town, lots of good guys there beat-
ing the clock. Come on by, there is a 2-for-1 this month.
Anything I can do for you, anytime, just call…"

Pain-crusted with cynicism and calluses,
thirty-eight years you existed within a withered body—
waited for a miracle to loose your limbs
from the filthy mat beside the pools of Bethesda.
Did you see an angel who came to stir the waters
or jealously watch for the sudden moving of the surface?
Did you calculate the season—or, as in all of life—
was it only when the wind moved?

Hope fluttered in your mind like a Roman flag
on the Praetorian wall as you watched
the blind see and the sick made whole—
whoever reached the trembling water first.
Why only one?
Is faith always singular, never plural?

Salvation came to visit you like a Sabbath breeze—
an exultation of larks overhead
and the flag caught the morning…
He asked the penetrating question,

"Do you want to get well?"

Your answer was crusted with explanation and excuse—
weak legs, troubled water, and the others had helpers.
You knew not who stood before you.
Compassion spoke again, a quiet, compelling voice—
no more excuses.

Faith broke through cynicism and calluses.
You stood straight on crippled legs.
No angel—
no water—
no helper—
only the healing Word.

John 5

Zacchaeus

He was not a very popular man in Jericho because he was the tax collector. He was able to skim off whatever extra he could squeeze from the townspeople as he collected for the Roman government. Tour guides still show you a Sycamore tree today in Jericho, as you stand in the shade sipping the world's best orange juice. Zacchaeus needed a safe place above the crowd so he scrambled up the tree to watch for Jesus. He had few friends to come to visit. No wonder his wife was caught off guard when he brought Jesus home for lunch. I think she exclaimed to her husband…

You short straw!

You squashed fig!

You stunted stick!

You brought *who* to stay at my house?
He invited Himself?
He insisted?
He saw you in the Sycamore tree,
the Sycamore tree?

You ripped your robe!

You runted goat!

You overgrown child!

You changed man…
what did He say
to you?

Luke 19

J.C.P.D.

We all depend on our police force to keep our cities safe. Television shows like *N.Y.P.D.* and *L.A. Law* draw huge followings. The battle between good and evil is constant. Our law keepers and tipsters identify dangerous criminals, try them, and put them behind bars, to our relief. Jerusalem was a hard city to govern under Roman occupation. Pilate tried his best to keep order at the behest of Caesar in distant Rome. It was considered a hardship post. Pilate and his wife longed to return to Rome and be done with these fractious Jews. They governed themselves with a 71-member body called the Sanhedrin, a two-party system of Pharisees and Sadducees who watched and reported on each other. Jesus came into this melee, disturbing all of the authorities, both Jewish and Roman, by His audacious statements about the temple, salvation, and His kingdom. Imagine with me two Roman soldiers of the J.C.P.D. reporting for duty…

"Why didn't you arrest Him?"

Two officers shifted on their legs like swaying wheat.
The older man stared straight ahead, his medals
for meritorious service shining like the sun—
"He said such wonderful things!"
"Wonderful—is He going to pay your salary too—
you gullible swine?"

"He said He was the bread of life and living water…"
"I've a good mind to put you on bread and water,
and see how you fare, but I can't spare even incompetent
fools,
the city is too restless."

The younger man offered, "Everyone was listening
to Him."
"Why didn't you bring Him in here to answer my ques-
tions?
You two are supposed to be the finest in all
of Jerusalem,
assigned to protect the Temple,
and you act like truant schoolboys."

"But He helped a crippled woman up to pay her tax,
praised her for giving all she had
then sat close to the women's court,
so they could listen to His teaching too."

"He is very kind."

"You fools,
He has no right to teach in our Temple,
which of our Jerusalem schools did He attend?"
"He said His teaching comes from God."
"That's blasphemy!"
"And that God sent Him…"
"I can't trust you to do your jobs anymore…"

"Sir, many in the crowd believed Him as their Messiah…"
"Soon the whole world will go after Him like stupid sheep
follow a Galilean shepherd. Messiah indeed!
Go back to your history books, you babies—
where will the Messiah come from?
Bethlehem, not Galilee!
Get out, go find another way to trap Him,
bribe someone if necessary."

Matthew

At that time Jesus said to the crowd, "Am I leading a rebellion, that you have come outwith swords and clubs to capture me? Everyday I sat in the temple courts teaching, and you did not arrest me."

Matthew 26:55

MALCHUS

Then Simon Peter, who had a sword, drew it and struck the high priest's servant [Malchus], cutting off his right ear.

John 18:10

Malchus Was Healed by the Messiah

He has shown you, O man, what is good.
And what does the Lord require of you?
To act justly and to love mercy
and to walk humbly with your God.

Micah 6:8

MALCHUS

It is remarkable that a Roman slave—even the High Priest's slave— should be mentioned at all, and by name, in a single verse of one of the most important stories of the Bible. Yet we might remember that it was Malchus who received Peter's impetuous strike that cut off his right ear. And the good Doctor Luke adds that Jesus healed him immediately. True to form, the young Mark, in his urgency to tell the Good News, just mentioned the ear, not the right ear. In fact all four Gospels mention this one little ear in an account packed with details. Fortunately for Peter, he was never charged with this action because of Christ's healing touch. In fact this was the last recorded miracle of the Master before the cross.

> Hey, Malchus,
> my friend Pat wants to find you
> to ask if you hear better
> with that ear…
> that ear…
> that Peter severed so savagely,
> like lightning splits
> a bruised sky.

Did you burn with sudden sounds
of the snake
shadowing the garden?

Your bloodied hands
fumbled with the ropes
trying to tie the Prisoner's hands…
those hands…
that touched your ear
with healing.
The Commander ordered haste
but the Jew did not struggle
to resist arrest.

You dared to look
into those sorrowful eyes…
those eyes…
that offered you
forgiveness.

Hey, Malchus,
Where are you?

The Gospels
John 18

PILATE

Herod Agrippa I, in a letter to Emperor Caligua, spoke of Pilate "As naturally inflexible, a blend of self will and relentlessness." Pilate had a thankless job in Judea, far from the authority and glamour of Rome, where the real decisions were made. His only hope was to keep these rabble-rousing crowds under control and then perhaps he would be recalled to his beloved city on seven hills and given a new white toga. But first he had to deal with this Jesus.

Pilate, what did you do after you condemned Him?
Pools of blood marred the Praetorian stones;
water spots dripped from guilty hands,
mute mockery in hours alone.
Soldiers hurried the raucous crowds away,
murderous shouts echoed in a throbbing head.
Your wife nowhere to be seen,
since she had warned of her dream.

A murder of crows darkened the morning
like clouds of torturous thoughts.
Black gloom shrouded your soul.
Cursing Caesar for this outpost of fractious Jews,
you paced the halls, passing mirrors winking back
blood-shocked eyes in a haggard face.

Lighted torches needed now at midday?
Had the world gone mad?
Suddenly—
the earth heaved—groaned—goblets shattered—
rocks split—the floor cracked—the air deathly still.

Where is a servant?
Send a message to Herod, (once enemy, now accomplice),
lounging in Tiberius by the inland sea, ask privately,
"What did you think of Him?"

Perhaps after the Passover Plot, (as some called it),
you fled to Caesarea by the great sea—linking to Rome—
but there was no peace in the palace.
Wind moaned—waves thrashed—crashed
on the rocks below your window, and
you were lonely in your bed.

Seeking distraction another day,
did you hurry to your reserved seat in the amphitheater,
only to see specters stalk upon that magnificent stage
with the sea backdrop?

Today, seeking anonymity,
you might escape to the green links beside the great blue sea.
But the little white ball still mocks like a mirror,
and your theatre seat is empty
in the British Museum's halls of ancient history.

The Gospels

So Pilate asked Jesus. "Are you the king of the Jews?"
"Yes, it is as you say," Jesusreplied. Then Pilate
announced to the chiefpriests and the crowd, "I find no
basis for acharge against this man."

Luke 23:3,4

THE CENTURION

A Centurion was hardened to hideous scenes like cruci-
fixion, the main form of execution by the Roman govern-
ment. This Jerusalem Centurion saw his distasteful job
as a necessary evil in order to be promoted someday. He
dreamed of being ordered to a Roman legion, perhaps to
sail the fresh breezes of the Mediterranean.

I serve Caesar.
I am loyal, rigorously trained, stronger than chains
that bind our prisoners, and proud to be born Roman.
Not like these poor, pitiful Jews that scurry
about these dusty streets like dogs, whimpering
every time I pass on my powerful horse, as if
I would ever bother with them at all.
I am assigned only to serve Pontus Pilate,
Governor of Judea.

This newest Prisoner must be extremely important—
arrested in the night and already sent to the Praetorian.
Make haste, my steed!
Whoa—Who is this?
Beaten bloody beyond recognition—
like fresh meat dripping at the butcher's stall—
He is a Jew, but why before Pilate?

I slapped His face for impudence—but—
O, His eyes—
Others plucked His beard—I—I could not—
but I spit upon Him in utter contempt.
O—but— His eyes were deep pools of sorrow.
I pressed a royal robe upon His raw shoulders, but
there was no anger in His eyes.

All the tortured way to the place of the skull
He never spoke, groaned, yes, but never
complained under the agony of the cross.
The jeering crowd mocked, cursed and reviled Him.

I choked on the dust, wiped horror from my face,
clutched my raging belly.
I held the nails—
the hammer blows struck—one—two—three.
Stumbling aside, I embarrassed myself in the weeds.
He spoke from the cross—guttural words, piercing words,
of the Father, Thirst, and Forgiveness.
O, His eyes—His eyes locked with mine—

Now, I serve the Crucified Christ.
I am loyal, rigorously forgiven,
stronger than chains which bound
my soul, and humbled to be a follower of this Jew.

Matthew 27

Thomas Everyman

You, Thomas, disciple of Jesus, asked the questions that so many people need answered. And you had been with Him three years, walked, talked, ate, and witnessed His miracles. With a knowing smile He had given you a basket of leftover bread and fish for your family. You were there when the lame walked and the blind saw. And yet—yet— belief came hard, like sleeping on rocky ground and not feeling rested. And now you decided you would not believe unless you could actually touch His wounds.

You must be cousin to everyone.
So many claim to be like you,
full as sunrise of doubt and fear,
uncertain what the day may bring.
When night falls they hide their heads
under pillows of piety, blankets of blindness,
claiming they will not believe unless they see.
Poor relations, these, to charge
their doubts to your overdrawn account.

For you, Thomas, had followed Him
some three years through storms and starlight.
Why? Why were you not with the Brothers
in fellowship when He came?
Doubt? Dread? Discouragement?
Even for Disciples? Yes,
we too know these Demons well.
You were not chided by the Lord
for questions, but for absence.

You missed rejoicing with friends
when He appeared fresh from the Tomb!
You missed His blessing of the Passover Peace!
You missed the Dedication Commissioning
when Jesus breathed His Holy Spirit power into them!

Eight days later you brought your questions
inside the locked door. Questions
do not negate faith, rather,
answered questions validate trust.
Trust—the first, the fiery, and final steps of faith.

In loving kindness Jesus appeared again,
extended scarred hands directly to you.
Falling at His pierced feet—you knew the answer
to all questions—
My Lord and My God!

John 20

Saul before the
Damascus Road

The damning text of Acts 7 tells of Saul, the Pharisee, holding the robes of the attackers when they murdered Stephen, the defender of the faith. Saul was one of the very best educated Jews of his day, a defender of the law, which he ardently believed was being blasphemed by the teachings of The Way. Zealous for the principles of his people, he was a crusader against heresy. Capable of terrible cruelty, he was possessed by burning hatred for all followers of this rebel rabbi. Much later the book of Hebrews tells us that Jesus is seated at the right hand of God, signifying His finished work. Stephen declared that he saw the heavens opened and the Son of God standing to receive him after his stunning testimony. Saul, surely the Savior stood up to receive you too, after you hung bloodied on that Roman cross. I wonder if the Messiah Jesus stands up to welcome all of His children home or especially those who have suffered great persecution, like martyrs and apostles. Saul, of course, becomes known as the Apostle Paul.

A murderous sneer scarred a handsome face,
mouth like a scimitar blade
as he guarded the tunics of the terrorists.
A strong sun on square shoulders
forged determination to iron.
On the rocky mountainside,
stone missiles glinted white and sharp.
A wake of Vultures hung in the weighted air.

Stephen, the accused, had argued a lengthy defense,
a thunder of ancient names
twisted somehow into new cloth until he
bound up Christ, that rebel rabbi,
with Israel's venerated Kings.

You, Saul, a student of Gamaliel,
knew the Law, seized the duty
to fight this new Way,
this pitiful rabble of believers
growing like barley in a newly ploughed field.

You resumed raiding their homes,
dragging them all away to prison,
men and women alike;
surprise attacks cut them down,
their screams and cries
discordant music to your ears.

Acts 6

PAUL

Paul, apostle, giant of God, I have been reluctant to address you. My pen does not know such depths of passion, nor heights of persuasion, nor grief nor pain as yours. I wonder at those who knew you then, drawn irresistibly by your words and work—Timothy, Claudia, Aquila, Priscilla, Luke, Peter—O, to have listened through a crack in the door to such conversations. I like to imagine the piercing hour when you ran gnarled fingers through tangled hair and clasped that helmet of salvation to your head.

Under the saffron sun we trudged ahead,
eyes downcast against the dangers of the road—
sharp stones that cut like a whip and tiny rocks
stuck in hot sandals like annoying conscience pricks.
Little conversation, now, in the acrid air,
venomous threats dried on parched lips.
Dust stung our eyes like angry bees.

No sign yet of the great Syrian city,
it must have moved perversely farther north.
No fig tree to offer merciful relief,
or sweet fruit to soften the murderous mouth
we would have welcomed even the scant shade
of a boulder under that relentless sun.

Hatred for those Jesus freaks drove him like a goad.
Saul had official permission to search, arrest, and drag
back to Jerusalem any traitor Jews,
but would make them suffer first.
They were enemies of the law, the tradition—
disgusting…they deserved to die…
like their hapless leader, Jesus.

The sun hammered us like carpenter's nails
on scorched skin, blistering light poured like molten sun.
Suddenly, Saul stumbled, fell to his face,
clawed his eyes, licked the dust as if dead.
We heard a voice but saw no one in the searing light.
He moved, mumbled, made an effort to stand,
tears streaming from blind eyes…
Saul became Paul.

Today if you traveled from Jerusalem to Damascus,
you might slake your thirst at "The Vision" just outside
the ancient walls, before the street called Straight

Acts 9

ANANIAS

If you dared to travel to Damascus today, perhaps in search of the famous damascene jewelry and wood-work, beautifully crafted, like you want to sell in your fine shop in Detroit, I can imagine that you would walk the ancient street called Straight, now crowded with Chevrolets and camels. You might actually walk where the Apostle Paul stumbled along as he was led by his friends, because of his sudden blindness. If God whispered your name in the cacophony of strange sounds, would you listen, would you respond, or would you hurry along your way, intent on making the very best business deal? After all, you don't remember that God ever spoke to you at home, well, maybe once or twice…

Ananias of Damascus,
powerful capital of Syria.
Well-known citizen, respected
in the bustling international marketplace,
A disciple of the Resurrected Messiah.

God moved you beyond your comfort zone.
Called you by name.
You answered as the prophet Samuel,
"Here I am, Lord."

It is always risky to
make yourself available
to God.

Sent to the street called Straight,
crossroad of the pulsing city,
to search for the house where
the infamous persecutor,
Saul of Tarsus, waited.
You found a blind man
who had seen true Truth.

Your fears fell like the scales from his eyes—
as stretching forth your hands to touch him—
each of you was healed.

I wonder if a man called Ananias
lives today in Damascus,
powerful capital of Syria?
Or, if he listens for the voice of the Lord,
would search the street called Straight
to find a man of God who speaks truth?
A man of the cross,
not of the crescent moon.

Acts 9

Cornelius

Someone has wisely said, "If you find the perfect church, don't join it; you will spoil it." Dissension within the church has always been a grave concern. Peter returned to Jerusalem to tell his fellow believers such wonderful news about his three days as a guest in Cornelius's home in Caesarea, a Gentile home, a Roman home, an enemies' home. Immediately the naysayers within the circle rebuked Peter, criticized his actions, wagged their baptized tongues, and pointed fingers at him. They snatched the joy and held it hostage. Peter carefully recounted the entire event until they changed their minds. Why are we often so quick to criticize our community of faith?

Did you consider the land of the Via Maris a hardship post?
You and your band of 100 Italians longed
to march from the port of Ostia
right up to the Roman Forum,
expecting special recognition since you
served so far from home.
At least it was magnificent Caesarea,
you and your wife attended concerts in Herod's amphitheater,
received invitations to Pilate's lavish parties.

God watched your kindnesses to family, soldiers, and friends.
His angel called you by name in a vision, one sleepless night.
You, a man of authority, quaked in the brilliant presence of
the divine messenger, weighing his unusual order.
Immediately you dispatched two faithful servants
and a soldier to guard them on the Via Maris,
the way of the sea,
down to Joppa to fetch a man called Peter.

Simon the tanner's house would be somewhere close
to the sea for fresh breezes to clear the rancid air.
Why would anyone want to stay there?
You had instructions to bring Peter to your home,
would a Jew stay with a Gentile and be made unclean?
On the way Peter told of a dream with beasts and fowls.

You welcomed him and talked far into the night,
as the waves whispered outside your window.
Talk of Jesus as the ultimate authority brought
you to your knees before dawn.
The Roman Centurion bowed before the Jewish
fisherman, and together you praised God.

Acts 10

AGABUS

No one likes bad news, much less the bearer of bad news. The Holy Spirit prompted you to warn and solicit help from the distant believers in Antioch for your brothers in Jerusalem. Not a popular request— there are so many worthy needs in the world, how is one to discern where help is needed the most? Blessings on those who dare to tell it like it really is and blessings on those who respond willingly.

You traveled a weary distance from
Jerusalem to Antioch.
A heavy heart your baggage,
to be opened before the fledgling church
in the aristocratic city of Antioch.
Would they believe you to be a prophet of God?
Fear clung like a wet cloak.
Would they disregard the warnings
like clouds before a raging storm?
Had love grown cold and prayer shriveled away
for those still in Jerusalem
after the sensorial stoning of Stephen?

The Brothers of Antioch took the cloak,
relieved you of the weighty baggage,
positioned you by the fire
and heeded your words of warning.
Generously they prepared a relief fund,
dispatched Barnabas and Paul before the
prophesied famine gripped the land
in the reign of Claudius Caesar.

Do we recognize God's prophets today
traveling our world with urgent words
warning of judgments yet to come?
Prophecies of war, famine, pestilence, and death;
four horsemen mounted to ride.
Clouds armed with hail lower the horizon.

Is prayer our priority?
Are we interceding for wisdom for the world's leaders?
Will we continue to give generously to relief funds
as those who were first to be called Christians?
As we are rebuffed by those who seized upon
our former aid, dangerous cold threatens our love.

Agabus, your name nearly forgotten,
your message needed yet again.
O God, help us to listen.
A Claudius Caesar may reign again.

Acts 11

Barnabas

I had the great privilege to attend a Middle Eastern conference on prayer as a delegate from North America. Three hundred and fifty women gathered from all over the area on the little island of Cyprus. For many it was the first time they had ever flown, or for some the very first time that they had ever been away from home. Fear, uncertainty, and timidity, crowded the hotel meeting room. Most everyone needed a headphone for translation. Gradually barriers were broken down as together we knelt before the throne of Grace. New understanding of one another, friendship, and trust grew daily. We did have a luscious lunch one day on the breezy beach and talked of Barnabas, who owned property on his home island of Cyprus. He is called the encourager and known as the travel companion of the Apostle Paul.

At the end of the week, as we all knelt on the marble floor, a local priest conducted a most meaningful communion service. Amidst tears and warm embraces, Vonette Bright, cofounder with her husband Bill, of

Campus Crusade for Christ, and organizer of this momentous event, offered this benediction: "We may never see one another again, here on earth, but when we get to heaven, let's all agree to meet at Paul's house."

Barnabas, where was the property that you sold,
on the windward or leeward side
of the almond-shaped island of Cyprus?
And your livelihood—fisher-
man, farmer, or merchant.?
O, to sit across a little beach table from you,
feet in the sand, shaded by a white umbrella,
listening to the music of the Mediterranean,
eating fish that swam but an hour ago,
and salt you with questions, Barnabas the encourager.

Was the wind strong the first day
that you boarded a ship
in Paphos for the journey of several days to Joppa,
in the beautiful land and on up the hills, until
you reached the high wall of Jerusalem?

Entering her Joppa gate, the cacophony of sounds
must have assaulted ears tuned to
the whistle of seagulls:

peddlers with push carts hawking their wares, wheels
clattering over cobblestones, the braying of animals,
iron clanging iron in the blacksmith's shop, coins
ringing in a ceramic dish, and the confusion of languages.
Children playing hide-and-seek
in the labyrinth of shops and narrow alleyways.

Ripe smells new to a nose trained to salt air:
oranges in the sun, coffee roasting in small copper pans,
big baskets of figs and dates oozing juice,
bread carried on the baker boy's
head, women hurrying
to put their pots of meat and vegetables
in the glowing coals of the baker's oven.

Passover time in Jerusalem.
You must have prayed with the Disciples,
debated long hours into the night
the implications of the Messiah's commands.
It was a significant sacrifice
to sell your quiet land at home
and give the money for missions.
Little did you dream that soon
you, Barnabas of Cyprus, and Paul of Tarsus,
a city far to the north, would sit at a little beach table,

feet in the sand of Paphos, shaded by a white umbrella,
listening to the music of the Mediterranean
and eat fish that swam but an hour ago,
all because the Master said,
"Go."

Acts 4

The Philippian Jailer

Magistrates and multitudes of people were milling about in the crowded streets of Philippi. The jailer raises his hand to speak about the uproar last night in his city regarding Paul and Silas: I will let the jailer speak for himself.

"Dear Citizens;
Please let me explain!
We are the chief city of Macedonia and a Roman colony.
Our jail, double-walled, is set outside the city gates
for keeping undesirables like those rabble-rousing Jews.
inexplicably staying at Lydia's home!"

"Multitudes charged that these two men, seemingly
itinerant religious men of some strange sect,
had been seen down by the riverside practicing
prayer and an odd ritual.
Now, upsetting business is intolerable!"

"Rip off their robes, bind them to the post,
begin the whipping!"
Was it the allowed 39 lashes, 40 known to be lethal?
As each stinging strip of leather
tied with metal bit into their backs,
multitudes and magistrates roared approval.
"Throw them into the inner cells, feet chained."
As if they could have managed to walk unaided.
"Satiated, I slept."

"Later, I learned that slumped on that filthy floor,
bloodied backs bent, they sang praises to their God
who certainly could not protect them from
our multitudes and magistrates..
Louder then, all the prisoners heard
the amazing balm of song,
stood straining to see these Jews."

"In the utter blackness of midnight
suddenly my bed heaved, the ground quaked,
walls buckled, water pots crashed,
and the iron gates swung open like freedom.
Distraught, I grabbed my sword to my heart.
A strong voice stayed my shaking hand.
"*We are all here*" Paul answered.

"I called for a light, ran stumbling,
and fell at their bruised feet,
What kind of God do you serve,
is there any hope for me,
how can I be saved?"

"The multitudes would demand my head.
God demanded my heart.
The prisoners bore me no malice,
spoke of love and forgiveness.
Wincing at their pain, I bathed their bloodied backs,
tears streaming from my eyes suddenly opening to the light."

"Tenderly I saw Paul and Silas to our home.
They told us of God Himself the Savior,
His beating on my behalf, His death for my sins,
His Resurrection for our hope and eternal life.
We all joined in Praise.
Gently as I had bathed their wounds
they baptized me and all my family
as we proclaimed our faith in the saving Christ."

"At first light the worried magis-
trates knocked at our door.
'*Let the prisoners go in peace*'
But Paul appealed to Caesar as a Roman citizen.
Fear struck the rulers like the quake.
I tell you, I saw the magistrates of our proud city
escort Paul and Silas past the silent
multitudes in the crowded street—
all the way back to Lydia's house.
Praise be to the God of my Salvation."

"We would be honored for you to visit our church,
the church of the Lord Jesus Christ,
dedicated to our first missionaries,
Paul and Silas."

Acts 16

APOLLOS

A very popular professor always has a following of students wanting to get into his classes. But some teachers have a wider experience and more information. They can expand open minds to understand greater realities of the same truth. Such was the relationship of Paul to Apollos. They were allies not adversaries.

"I am of Apollos," the people cried.
You did not seek such accolades,
you were of the Messiah,
as the grape is of the vine.
New wine flowed
in veins long narrowed by tradition;
belief had been based on limited knowledge,
like the juice of only a small portion of the vineyard.

Citizen of Alexandria,
that city of such lugubrious days and balmy nights
that they employ no word for weather,
always the perfect temperature to ripen swelling fruit.

You sailed to Ephesus—business or pleasure?
Paul had harvested the fruit of the Holy Spirit,
was busy filling new skins with new wine—
the powerful result after days and nights
of prayerful preaching.

Your trained mind was good soil for cultivation.
Knowing only the baptism of John,
you spoke boldly in the synagogue, of repentance,
gathering only small fruit as if not yet mature.
Priscilla and Aquilla, the tentmakers,
invited you home for dinner.
They husbanded your fertile mind,
befriending you like rain and sun for growth.
Until the day you left for Acacia with a letter
of recommendation to the brethren Jews,
and new vineyards were planted.
Not by Paul, or Apollos
but by the Holy Spirit of Christ,
the Risen Messiah.

Acts 18

Tertius

The computer programmer is never as well known as the creator of the text, or the secretary of the boss, nor does the law clerk get the recognition of the lawyer, and neither does the layout designer get adequate praise for making the book readable. The Apostle Paul always acknowledged by name those who so greatly assisted him in getting out the Good News about the risen Christ, such as Tertius who served as his amanuensis. Who remembers Lucius, Jason, Sosipater, Gaius, Erastus, Quartus, in the letter to the Romans? Stephanas, Fortunatus, and Achaicus supplied his need and refreshed his spirit, and Titus and Lucas recorded his advice to the Corinthians. Galatians he wrote with his own hand. Was there no one to help him at that time in Rome? The letter to the Ephesians he entrusted to Tychicus, a beloved brother. The book good for mental health, Philippians, comes to us by Epaphroditus from Rome. Colossians commends Tychitus, Onesimus, Aristarchus, Marcus, Justus, and Nymphas who hosted a house church, Epaphrus who prayed, and Luke whom we know for his meticulous account of our Lord's life. But whatever happened to Demas?

Greetings to you, Tertius, I am writing to you in appreciation for your faithful service to Paul.

You had learned to listen carefully.

Did your pen not flame with the fire of his heart pouring liquid silver wisdom onto the thirsty parchment?

Did you dip again and again and yet again into the Truth ink to inscribe clearly his treatise?

Exact skills were required in spelling and legibility so the molten words would flow and solidify into precious Gospel gold.

The Jew and Gentile would know of God's grand provision for them.

Nuggets of Salvation, Grace, and Faith shine with incandescent beauty in a darkening world. Justification and Sanctification ring like bronze bells over a fragmented earth. Doctrine is delivered with strong links forged of Redemption and Resurrection.

You, Tertius, copied exactly the molded teachings of the Law and the Prophets when Paul tugged on his aging beard and quoted timeless Truth. We know nothing of your preparation for this trusted position, but it is enough to know that Paul placed his confidence on your strong shoulders to etch enduring gold.

Thank you for your faithful service,
Alegria
Romans 16

DEMAS

I have never heard of anyone named Demas. No parent would give a son that infamous name if he knew the meaning. We make up new names, or rely on strong names of honor to pass from generation to generation. We revere ancestors who were wonderful role models, or men who accomplished great things. But we know of no other Judas or Demas.

Was it *Maxim* or *Playboy*
that caught your eye…flash of color or skin…
as you wiped the sweat from your brow?

The sun high, like a molten vat of oil
ready for the head of the enemy.
Sandal calluses rubbed over
endless miles on tired feet.
Linen tunic plastered to strong body
conditioned by arduous travel with Paul.

Was it Rome or Corinth
that shouted to your hammering heart,
causing you to stumble?

You had started well, been invited by Paul
to be a worthy companion in running the race.
Each milepost strengthened the bond
of fellow servants, your trusted name
even listed as sending greetings with his.

Was it doubt or Thessaloniki
that drew you away, like precious water
leaking from a damaged goatskin?

Did you go home,
or to gamble, or
visit houses of nightfall
that caused you to become
a caustic critic of the New Way?

It matters not,
except your once proud,
polished name will forever mean
Demas the deserter.

II Timothy 4

TIMOTHY

Did your dad die young? Many good men do. Was he consumed by effort to provide for his family, or did he run away from responsibility at home, for greener pastures, leaving you in the care of two very strong women? They were strong because they were characterized by prayer—your mother, Eunice, and grandmother, Lois. Someone noted that if you have a grandmother praying for you, you will do well. How like God to give you an extraordinary role model, the Apostle Paul as your mentor. And you were God's gift to the godly giant, he loved you and taught you lessons every son needs to know.

Timothy, where did you meet the Apostle Paul?
Was he debating in the shade of Solomon's porch,
or striding down David Street—embroidered cloak
billowing like the sail of a great ship bound for Rome,
spilling oranges in the market in his wake?
Did you match him stride for stride,
straining to follow animated reasoning,
answering countless questions,
defending your commitment?

Paul, did warn you of hardship and grace,
like two sides of the same coin—
one side a necessary payment to life,
the other, abundant grace in the storeroom
available for every situation you would ever face.

It is evident that Paul poured out
all the love for a son,
and all the passion of being imprisoned,
and all the joy of serving Christ,
like anointing oil on your young beard.

When fair winds rose,
you left the safe moorings together,
rose and fell with the moods of the sea.
Fresh winds and foul pushed you
toward study of ancient law,
new Resurrection truth,
and rhythms of rhetoric
in contemporary myths.

Satisfied,
Paul left you behind at Ephesus,
like good mentors must do,
in that teeming crossroads of Europe and Asia,
promising to write to you soon.

Timothy

Afterword

"The master works of God are those men who stand in the midst of difficulties, steadfast and unmovable."

—C.H. Spurgeon